◄ NATIVE AMERICAN PEOPLE ►

THE UTE

by Craig A. Doherty and Katherine M. Doherty

Illustrated by Richard Smolinski

ROURKE PUBLICATIONS, INC.

VERO BEACH, FLORIDA 32964

CONTENTS

Printed in the USA

Library of Congress Cataloging-in-Publication Data

Doherty, Katherine M.
    The Ute / by Katherine M. Doherty, Craig A. Doherty.
        p.   cm. — (Native American people)
    Includes bibliographical references.
    1. Ute Indians—Juvenile literature. I. Doherty, Craig A.
II Title. III. Series.
E99.U8D65 1994   970.004'974—dc20   93-37999
ISBN 0-86625-530-3   CIP
                                                                    AC

Introduction

For many years archaeologists—and other people who study early Native American cultures—agreed that the first humans to live in the Americas arrived about 11,500 years ago. These first Americans were believed to have been big-game hunters. They lived by hunting the woolly mammoths and giant bison that inhabited the Ice Age plains of the Americas. This widely accepted theory also asserted that these first Americans crossed a land bridge linking Siberia, in Asia, to Alaska. This land bridge occurred when the accumulation of water in Ice Age glaciers lowered the level of the world's oceans.

In recent years, many scientists have challenged this theory. Although most agree that many big-game hunting bands left similar artifacts all over the Americas 11,500 years ago, many now suggest that the first Americans may have arrived as far back as 20,000 or even 50,000 years ago. There are those who think that some of these earliest Americans may have even come to the Americas by boat, working their way down the west coast of North America and South America.

In support of this theory, scientists who study language or genetics (the study of the inherited similarities and differences found in living things) believe that there may have been more than one period of migration. They

also believe that these multiple migrations started in different parts of Asia, which accounts for the genetic and language differences that exist among the people of the Americas. Although it is still not certain when the first Americans arrived, scientists agree that today's Native Americans are descendants of early Asian immigrants.

Over the thousands of years between the first arrivals from Asia and the introduction of Europeans, the people who were living in the Americas flourished and inhabited every corner of the two continents. Native Americans lived above the Arctic Circle in the North, to Tierra del Fuego at the tip of South America, and from the Atlantic Ocean in the East to the Pacific Ocean in the West.

During this time, the people of North America divided into hundreds of different groups. Each group adapted to the environment in which it lived. As agriculture developed and spread throughout the Americas, some people switched from being nomads to living in one area. Along the Mississippi River, in the Southwest, in Mexico, and in Peru, groups of Native Americans built large cities. In other areas, groups continued to exist as hunters and gatherers with no permanent settlements. One group of Native Americans who continued a nomadic lifestyle was the Ute.

Origins of the Ute

Native Americans are grouped together by their languages. One large family of Native American languages, Uto-Aztecan, was spoken from Central America north to what is now

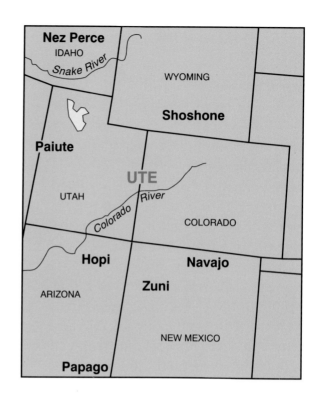

Idaho. The Aztecs spoke one language from this family, and the Ute spoke another. Although their languages were from the same family, these two peoples were not able to understand each other. The Ute would, however, have been able to understand other Uto-Aztecan languages spoken by tribes that lived near to them. Both the Paiute and the Shoshone, for example, were tribes that could communicate with the Ute. They all spoke a branch of Uto-Aztecan called Numic.

The Ute took their name from the Native American word *Eutaw* or *Yuta*, which means "dwellers in the tops of mountains." In English, this became Utahs. Then in the nineteenth century, the Utah tribe was called the Ute. When Europeans arrived in this part of North America, the Ute ranged over a vast territory. Their lands included most of present-day Utah and the mountainous regions of Colorado. This area is part of the Great Basin.

Where the Ute came from, and when they arrived in North America, are questions that are still discussed among scientists. The most likely explanation is that they arrived in the Great Basin area in about 1000 A.D. A group of people, called the Fremonts, lived in this region before the Ute. Archaeological evidence indicates that the Fremont people were in decline and the Ute took over their territory.

Although much of this territory is barren desert, the Ute were able to collect and hunt all they needed in order to survive.

Daily Life

The Ute were divided into bands. A band is a subdivision of a tribe. At one time, there were eleven different Ute bands. The housing each band built was varied, depending on the materials available. Those who had contact with the Shoshone, and other Plains Indians to the east, adopted the *tipi* as their main form of housing. Other bands built domed structures of willow branches over a pole frame. These willow domes were probably the more traditional Ute dwelling. Since the Ute moved every season to hunt and collect food, their homes were temporary.

A Ute willow dome shelter was approximately eight feet high and fifteen feet in diameter. Four poles were used for a frame, with one end of each pole buried in the ground. The poles then had to be bent down and lashed together in order to form a dome. Willow boughs were then attached to the frame to form the roof and walls. Some Ute bands built dome shelters and covered them with bark, brush, or reeds. The Ute did not leave a smoke hole in their dome shelters.

The Ute who adopted the *tipi* from the Plains Indians, used elk or buffalo skins as coverings. Those Ute living closest to the plains, where buffalo were plentiful, used buffalo skins; those living in the mountains were more likely to use elk skins. It usually took between six and ten hides to make a *tipi.* The Ute probably started using *tipis* after they acquired horses. The *tipi* covers were too heavy to move without the help of horses.

Whether a band used traditional dome shelters or *tipis,* their camps were similar. They usually set up their camps in a river or stream valley. Their shelters were scattered to take advantage of available wood for cooking and the shade of the trees. Winter camps were often at lower elevations, due to the milder weather there.

Three Ute women attach a tipi *covering to its frame.*

Family Life

Children were highly valued among the Ute people. Everyone in the camp shared the responsibility of caring for and educating the children. Cradle boards were often used to hold babies. Some Ute built a cradle board of willow branches that included a hood to shade the baby's head. Others used the more common solid-wood cradle boards, probably adopted from the Plains Indians. Willow bark was often used for diapers.

Babies were frequently cared for by girls who were nine or ten years old. These baby-sitters either carried the cradle boards or strapped them to their backs. Both Ute boys and girls were expected to begin helping with the food-collecting duties of the camp as soon as they were able.

Ute women delivered their children in special birthing shelters. Their husbands were expected to provide lots of firewood to keep the mothers warm during labor and delivery. A woman about to give birth was usually assisted by one of her female relatives. During pregnancy and an infant's very early months, a mother followed certain tribal taboos. A taboo is a rule that forbids specific actions, with the intent of preventing certain problems. Most

Opposite: A willow dome shelter is constructed. Below: Babies were kept secure in their cradle boards.

of the Ute taboos that affected pregnant women involved staying away from particular foods during pregnancy.

When a child was born, the umbilical cord was cut with a stone knife. When the remaining part of the cord had dried and fallen off, the mother always saved it. The cord was put in a special pouch that was often attached to the baby's cradle board. When the baby was able to walk, the mother would dispose of the cord, usually onto a red anthill. It was believed that by giving the baby's cord to the ants, some of the ants' industriousness would rub off on the child.

Among the Ute, twins were considered to be bad luck, born because of inappropriate behavior by the parents. If twins were born, one or both twins was usually allowed to die.

Many Ute had a number of names and nicknames. Often a child was given one name at birth and another when he or she learned to walk. A Ute's name might change again, according to his or her accomplishments. In addition to a formal name, a Ute frequently had more than one nickname.

There do not seem to have been any formal ceremonies to mark puberty among the Ute people. Young women were, however, kept in a separate hut while they were menstruating. They were expected to follow certain dietary restrictions during this time and avoid contact with hunters and people who were sick. After their first menstruation, young women were permitted to participate in the annual Bear Dance. It was during this dance that men and women found their spouses.

The annual Bear Dance ceremony.

Young boys also did not have a ceremony to mark their passage through puberty. However, they did follow some taboos. One taboo was that a young man was forbidden to eat any of the first big-game animal that he killed.

There was no formal education among the Ute. Children learned to survive by watching and helping their elders. Finding and preparing food was the most important and time-consuming activity of the Ute. Children helped in any way they could. As they learned new tasks, they were given more responsibility.

Food Gathering and Preparation

For the Ute, everything they needed to survive could be collected in their territory. There were some differences between what various Ute bands ate. Those in the western part of the Ute territory tended to eat more plant foods, while those in the eastern part depended more on hunting large animals. Anthropologists have only found evidence that the Ute briefly practiced agriculture.

The list of plants that the Ute used is long. One major food source came from the nuts found in the pinecones of the piñon pine tree. There were thick piñon forests in the higher elevations throughout the Ute range, and although the new harvest varied greatly from year to year, enough piñon groves existed so that the Ute gatherers had plenty of supplies.

During the piñon-gathering time, the whole camp would move to the piñon forests, and stay there until they were

driven to lower elevations by snow or cold weather. It was important to get to the nuts, which fall out of their cones when ripe, before the squirrels and other animals did. To accomplish this, Ute hunters used long sticks to knock the nuts down from the trees.

During the piñon harvest, many of the men spent time hunting deer, which resulted in a Ute diet that consisted almost exclusively of piñons and

Opposite: Pottery vessels and baskets were used to cook soups and stews. Below: A Ute woman named Chipeta is surrounded by woven cooking baskets.

venison during the harvest season. In a year of abundant piñons, the fall harvest had a very partylike atmosphere. Many trips were made to carry the extra piñon nuts to the winter camp. Large quantities of piñons were stored for the winter.

In addition to piñon nuts, the Ute collected a number of different wild foods. Grass seeds were used in the same way as modern, farm-raised grains. Berries were collected in season, and what wasn't eaten fresh was dried to be added to foods during the winter. Wild potatoes and other roots were gathered and eaten, as well as a number of wild greens. One plant that all Ute used every part of was the yucca. Its blossoms and fruit were eaten, its roots were used to make

soap, and its leaves provided long fibers that were woven into a number of useful items, including sandals.

The Ute also gathered one plant that was not for eating—wild tobacco. Tobacco was important to many Native Americans, who smoked it as part of their religious and social obligations. The Ute discovered that wild tobacco often grew in abundance in areas where there had been a fire. It is believed that the Ute would deliberately burn off an area to encourage tobacco growth.

The Ute people prepared the food they collected in a variety of ways. Various roots were often baked in earthen ovens or eaten raw. Many types of foods were dried. Meats were either roasted over an open fire or cut into thin strips and dried, to be added later to soups and stews. Berries were made into cakes that were often enhanced with dried crickets or grasshoppers. Piñon nuts were eaten raw and also stored for later use. Dried piñon nuts were ground into flour.

Stews and soups were staples of the Ute diet. Various grains, berries, roots, meats, and fish were combined. The western bands of Ute had pottery vessels for cooking their stews and soups directly over fires. The eastern bands did not use pottery. Instead, they cooked in coiled baskets. To cook in a basket, a Ute would take a hot stone from the fire and add it to whatever food was in the basket. The basket was kept moving so the stone would not burn it. Using cooking stones was a common practice among Native Americans who did not use pottery.

To store food, the Ute built platforms in evergreen trees. The thick growth of the branches above the platform protected the food. They also dug pits, lined them with bark or grass, and then filled them up with sacks of roots, nuts, seeds, and other dried food. The pits were then covered with rocks and dirt and a fire was built over the pit to camouflage its scent. Even so, bears sometimes found, and dug up, the Ute's stored food.

Hunting and Fishing

Although the Ute men helped with the collection of plant foods during the busiest times, their main activity was providing meat. The Ute lived in one of the most game-rich areas of western North America. Buffalo, elk, whitetail deer, mule deer, antelope, mountain sheep, moose, jackrabbits, cottontail rabbits, and many other mammals were hunted and eaten. The Ute also fished a number of rivers and lakes in their territory, hunted birds, and collected insects to eat.

The bow and arrow was the primary hunting tool of the Ute, who used both wooden and horn bows three to four feet in length. Horn bows were made by heating and straightening the horn of a mountain sheep. The horn was then split and shaped. Once the bow maker had the right shape, he would wrap the bow with sinew (tendons) to give it strength. Arrows were about two feet long, and those used on big game had stone arrow points. For small game, hunters fire-hardened the end of the shaft and sharpened it.

Ute hunters often stalked big-game animals by themselves, but they also worked together to drive animals into a narrow area where they could more easily shoot them with their bows. Sometimes the Ute hunters built two long fences of brush, set up to form a funnel. Antelope and other game would be driven into the wide end of the fences, while more hunters waited at the narrow end of the fences to kill the animals.

In the winter, large herds of elk would come down out of the mountains. Ute hunters on snowshoes often surrounded a herd, which could not escape in the deep snow. In this way, they easily harvested the animals they needed. The Ute also had rabbit drives. The western bands used nets, while the eastern bands killed the rabbits with bows and clubs.

Birds were hunted in a number of ways. Waterfowl were often driven

A young boy finishes making an arrow with a stone point.

into shallow marshes, at a time before the young of the year could fly and the adults were molting and were unable to fly. Waterfowl eggs were also an important source of food in the early spring. Other birds were shot with special arrows, which had a forked-stick point. Sage grouse were often netted when they went to a water hole to drink in the early morning or late afternoon.

The lakes, rivers, and streams of the Great Basin still offer some of the best fishing in the West. The Ute developed several ways to catch fish. They speared them, as well as shot them with special barbed fish arrows. Fish were also trapped in weirs and nets. A fish weir was made by blocking a river with brush or rocks, and forcing the fish to swim through a narrow opening in the weir. Fish could then be easily netted or speared as they swam through the weir. The Ute were also very good at catching fish using only their hands.

In the winter, the Ute frequently built shelters directly on the frozen lakes and ponds. Inside these shelters, holes were then cut in the ice and fish were able to be caught with a bow and arrow, or a spear.

Ute hunters used snowshoes in the winter to be able to move more easily in the snow as they hunted elk and other game.

Below: A young hunter in traditional dress with his bow and arrow. Opposite: A Ute woman in decorative traditional dress.

Clothing

The Ute dressed simply. As contact with the Plains Indians increased, however, the eastern Ute bands began to decorate their clothing in the style of the Plains Indians. Most Ute men dressed in a deerskin breechcloth, deerskin leggings, and moccasins or sandals. Deerskin shirts were also worn when needed.

The Ute moccasins were made of two pieces. The sole consisted of a tough leatherlike buffalo hide, while the upper was made of a softer leather such as elk or deer hide. Muskrat or beaver-skin insoles were often inserted into Ute moccasins. In the warmer months, the Ute wore sandals made from the fiber of the yucca plant.

Ute women wore skirts that were made of skins, or woven with bark or reeds, and that reached to the knees. Their deerskin leggings came up to just below their knees. Ute women also wore long dresses made from two doe-skins, which covered them from neck to ankle.

The Ute liked to wear jewelry and often wore small polished bones in their noses. Necklaces were also popular and were made of a variety of materials—animal claws, bone beads, stones, and various seeds. Decorative belts might be painted and include feathers. On special occasions, the Ute painted their faces with white, black, yellow, red, blue, and green face paints. For these special times they also decorated their hair with white and black paint and feathers.

The Ute also tattooed their faces. In order to do this, they first pierced their skin with sharp cactus thorns that had been dipped in a special mixture that was made with water and cedar-leaf ashes. The color of the ashes would then remain in the scar, thus creating the tattoo.

Games

Although collecting and hunting for food took up much of the Ute's time, they still enjoyed a number of games. Dice was particularly popular. The dice used were made of rectangular pieces of willow, one side flat and the other rounded. Both sides were painted with marks. The dice were thrown into a shallow tray or basket. The highest combination of marks determined the winner. Counting sticks were used to keep track of the score. The winner of each throw of the dice was awarded a stick. Both players and observers would bet on the outcome of the game.

Shinny, another favored game, was usually played by teams of ten to twenty-five women, with curved sticks and a ball. The playing field, approximately 250 feet long, had a goal at each end, and the object was to get the ball into the opponent's goal. The ball could either be hit with the stick or

Opposite: Two Ute men attempt to hit a rolling hoop in a game of darts. Above: A Ute doll was a popular toy that children enjoyed.

kicked. Sometimes the games would begin in the spring and be played every day for a month.

Another game that the Ute men enjoyed was a form of darts. In this game a hoop was used as the target, and was rolled along the ground. Points could be scored by hitting the rolling hoop or by having the hoop stop on your dart. A point could also be made if your dart was close to the place the hoop stopped. The hoop-and-dart game was usually played by two people at a time, though on occasion more would join in the fun. The score was kept with counting sticks.

Political and Social Organization

The political and social organization of the Ute was closely related. The Ute tribe was divided into eleven known bands. A band of Ute, which had its own territory, was divided into camps. Each camp was an independent unit. A camp was usually made up of a number of related families, following the family lines of the women. Camps consisted of 50 to 150 people, depending on the availability of food. Areas that had an abundance of food could support larger camps.

Within a camp, each household was somewhat independent, free to move about and to join another camp if they wished. But the members of the camp cooperated in gathering food, hunting, and fishing.

A camp leader was often the most successful hunter, chosen because of his ability to provide food. The camp would follow his lead as to when and

The Ute Chief Savara and his family, taken in 1899.

where to move. If a family was unhappy with the camp leader, they could leave and join a camp whose leader they liked. In this way, a strong leader usually ended up with a large camp. The Ute probably switched bands as well as camps, although for the most part people stayed within their groups.

There was little political or social interaction between the camps within a band, or between the bands. After the Ute acquired horses, however, raiding parties that represented one band would travel throughout the Southwest. War leaders became more important during this time.

Within the camps it was important that the Ute kept their relations straight. They had separate words to name their maternal and paternal grandparents. They also used special words that referred to the relative ages of their brothers and sisters.

Although the camps were independent, they did get together at least once a year. Toward the end of winter in late February or in early March, each band would hold an annual Bear Dance.

Religious Life

The Ute believed that long ago a Ute hunter had seen a bear come out of his winter den and dance. The bear told the hunter that if he would copy the bear's dance he would become a better hunter and a better husband. So each year the Ute gathered together and held their bear dances. A special brush enclosure was made by the group hosting the dance. The dance lasted for as long as ten days. During the dance, a group of Ute singers would sing the bear-dance songs and play a rasplike instrument.

The men and women of the tribes formed separate lines that faced each other and then selected a partner to dance opposite them. It was at the Bear Dance that young men and women would find a person to marry. During the Bear Dance, the people not dancing would visit with each other and gamble. At the end of the dance, the host group provided a feast for all those who had come.

The Ute believed their world had been created by a spirit who lived in the sky. This spirit, bored with its life, had drilled a hole through the bottom of the sky through which it could see a barren world below. The spirit sent snow and rain through the hole, which formed the mountains and rivers.

Next, the spirit decided to visit this newly formed world, but was disappointed because of its emptiness. To fix this, the spirit created plants, animals, and people. Because the spirit could not remain forever, it put a wise grizzly bear in charge of the world. All the creatures, except the coyote, always followed the grizzly's leadership.

Everything living in the world was believed to have a spirit, and the Ute respected all living things. They gave thanks to the spirit world when they were allowed a successful hunt. They also gave thanks when they were able to find enough plants to gather.

The Ute believed that certain members of their groups had an especially close connection to the spirit world. These people were their religious leaders, or *shamans*. Anthropologists have determined that there were an equal number of men and women who were *shamans* among the Ute.

When a Ute died, relatives would prepare the body for its journey to the spirit world. A Ute's body was always washed and dressed in the best clothing, and the face was painted. Usually, the Ute buried their dead, often in a cave or a crevice in the rocks. When a body was buried it always faced the east. On occasion, the Ute would cremate a body, and sometimes the home of the person who died was also burned. The surviving relatives often cut their hair short and did not participate in any dances for a year. The

Pages 24–25: The sky spirit looks down at the Earth below as described in the Ute creation legend.

23

spouse of the person who died was expected to wait for one year before remarrying.

The Ghost Dance movement began in the late 1800s in Nevada and spread east to the Plains tribes and others, including the Ute. The Ghost Dance represented the return of all the Native Americans who had died as a result of contact with non-Indians, and the removal of the Europeans from Indian territory. Much of this movement ended within a few years.

European Contact

During the sixteenth and seventeenth centuries, Spanish explorers and settlers moved northward from Mexico into what are today the states of Arizona, California, and New Mexico. The Spanish settlers had little direct contact with the Native Americans

who lived at a distance from their settlements. Although they tried to keep Native Americans from acquiring horses, by the middle of the seventeenth century the Ute bands in what is now southern Colorado were riding and raising them.

In 1680, the Pueblo people of the Rio Grande Valley in New Mexico revolted against the Spanish. The Spanish, forced to abandon their settlements in New Mexico and return to Mexico, left behind most of their livestock, including many horses. The horse changed the way of life for the Native Americans of the plains and for the Ute.

The horse made all of these people much more mobile. The ability to travel over great distances with ease affected the balance of space that had existed among the Native Americans. Plains Indians began to hunt on the lands of the eastern Ute. The Ute and other groups began to spend more of their time raiding each other and the European settlements. On their raids, they would steal horses. When raiding other Native Americans, the Ute and other tribes often took captives to sell to the Spanish. Before and after the Pueblo Revolt, when the Spanish returned to New Mexico, the Spanish used Native American slaves to work their farms and ranches.

The Spanish authorities tried to control the trade with Native Americans, but many traders defied the authorities because there was so much money to

be made in the illegal trade. Even though heavy trading was taking place between the Ute and the Spanish settlers in New Mexico, their contact was minimal. Until the nineteenth century, there were no attempts made by non-Indians to move onto Ute lands.

The first non-Indians to move onto Ute lands were mountain men intent on trapping and trading for valuable furs. The emphasis on fur-bearing animals quickly depleted this resource and changed hunting patterns. Many Native American hunters began hunting for furs instead of spending their time hunting for larger food animals. The goods they traded for—metal tools and weapons, jewelry, guns, and alcohol—changed their traditional way of life forever.

In 1821, after a long revolution, Mexico gained its independence from Spain. The Mexicans were more active in pursuing trade with the Ute. However, the first real loss of lands to whites came from people fleeing religious persecution in the United States. In 1847, Brigham Young and his Mormon followers arrived in the area of the Great Salt Lake. The Mormons chose this spot because it was then part of Mexico. They believed that they would be able to practice their religion without interference.

The Mormons picked their settlement location carefully. They chose an area that was not actively occupied by either the Ute to the south or the Shoshone to the north. It was the Mormons' policy to get along with their Native American neighbors. For the most part they were successful.

The Mexican-American War was the beginning of vast changes for the Native Americans of the Southwest. The United States defeated the Mexicans and forced them to sign the Treaty of Guadalupe Hidalgo in 1848. In this treaty, the Mexican government gave up its claim to what is now New Mexico, Arizona, California, Colorado, Utah, and Nevada. Shortly after the United States took over this territory, miners, ranchers, other settlers, and the U.S. Army arrived in huge numbers.

The ranchers and miners caused the biggest problems for the Ute. The ranchers' herds of cattle were put right on the land that was most needed by the Ute. The cattle ate or trampled the grass from which the Ute would have collected seeds. They also took over springs and other desirable sites near water. Miners ruthlessly claimed land that they believed had any valuable mineral resources. Mining camps sprang up all over Ute territory. The army took responsibility for protecting the interest of non-Indians whether they had legitimate claims to the land or not.

After living for almost 1,000 years in relative peace and harmony in the Great Basin, both the Ute's land and their way of life were lost over the span of one generation. European diseases, which Native Americans had no immunity to, killed many of the Ute. With the loss of their traditional way of life, the Ute became dependent upon the U.S. government for their survival. Indian agencies (organizations established by the United States to exert control over Native Americans) were set up to govern the Ute.

All throughout this time, the Ute continued to lose more and more of their traditional lands to non-Indian

This Ute woman, "Susan," helped white women who were held captive during the Meeker Massacre.

settlers. The Ute, like other Native American groups, tried to survive as best they could. Some Ute were pushed too far by the government officials. In 1878, Nathan Meeker became the Indian agent for the Ute reservation in Colorado. His strict ways caused some Ute to rebel. Colorow, the leader of the Ute, and Meeker did not get along. So Meeker appointed Sanovick, another Ute who was Colorow's rival, to be head of the tribe.

When this happened, Colorow and his followers began performing war dances in the streets of the agency. Meeker called for help from the army, and 175 soldiers from Fort Steele moved onto the Ute reservation. Colorow and his followers trapped the soldiers in Red Canyon for an entire week as they waited for reinforcements. Colorow, and his 70 warriors, killed 14 soldiers and wounded 43 others.

While the siege was under way in Red Canyon, other followers of Colorow attacked the agency. They killed Meeker, his family, and seven other whites. This event is referred to as the Meeker Massacre. Finally, 1,000 troops arrived on the Ute reservation and captured Colorow and his followers. After one more brief attempt at rebellion, Colorow and 1,500 other Ute were then moved from Colorado to the Unitah Reservation in Utah. The Unitah were one of the Ute bands.

At the beginning of the eighteenth century, the Ute controlled most of what is now Colorado and Utah. By the end of the nineteenth century, they had three small reservations, one in Utah and two in Colorado. Their lands were further reduced by the Dawes Act of 1887. The Dawes Act made provisions for taking all tribally held lands in the United States and allotting it to individual Native Americans. Any Indian land not allotted could be sold. Although the Ute fought allotment, they continued to lose more and more of their land.

The Ute Today

In 1990, according to the U.S. Census, there were 7,273 people who were counted as Ute. Of these, 2,279 lived in Colorado, 3,065 lived in Utah, and those remaining lived elsewhere in the United States. There are currently three Ute reservations: The Unitah Reservation, in Utah, and the Ute Mountain Reservation and the Southern Ute Reservation, in Colorado.

A large group of Ute men, women, and children gather for a photograph in 1907.

All three are remotely located, and their people are experiencing many of the same problems faced by other Native Americans living on reservations throughout the United States.

Poverty is the largest problem faced by the Ute. On the average, a Ute family has half the income of the average non-Indian in the United States. Unemployment is over fifty percent when it is adjusted to include those who find only seasonal work. Alcohol abuse is a serious problem.

There are also factional differences among the Ute. Ute who are from different bands have been forced to live in close proximity on lands that were not traditionally theirs. There is little opportunity for Ute who wish to stay on their reservations. They lack job-skills training and have a high-school dropout rate that is more than twice the national average. There are no short-term solutions to many of these problems.

Despite these problems, the Ute are working to hang onto their Native American heritage. On the Unitah Reservation, many Ute are learning to read and write in their native language. Among them, there is an increased awareness of the need for an education, and many are attending off-reservation high schools in an attempt to become better educated. Income from natural resources, and other leases of tribal lands, have given the Ute some funds to help with these problems.

The Ute Mountain Reservation recently opened a casino, and over eighty Ute are employed there. The casino has also boosted the economy of nearby Cortez, Colorado. In addition to the jobs generated, the casino has helped to improve relations between the Ute and the nearby non-Indian population. The Ute have reason to be guardedly hopeful about their future.

Chronology

1600s Eastern Ute make first contacts with Europeans.

1680 Pueblo Revolt occurs in New Mexico. The Spanish return to Mexico, leaving horses behind that are available to the Ute.

1821 Mexican Revolution ends and independence for Mexico is created, leading to more interaction between Ute and non-Indians.

1847 Brigham Young and his Mormon followers settle in Ute territory.

1848 Treaty of Guadalupe Hidalgo ends the Mexican-American War and gives the United States the lands that become the states of Colorado, New Mexico, Arizona, California, Nevada, and Utah.

1855 The Colorado Ute negotiate the treaties of *Abiquiu* with the governor of New Mexico.

1858 The Ute help the Mexicans and the Americans in their fight with the Navajo.

1868 Many of the Colorado Ute sign a treaty with the U.S. government in which 15 million acres are given up by the Ute.

1870 Many of the Ute in Utah participate in the Ghost Dance.

1878 Meeker Massacre, in which angry Ute kill the Indian Agent Nathan Meeker, his family, and 7 other whites. After the incident, 1,500 Ute are moved from Colorado to Utah.

1882 A reservation is started and many Ute are forced to relocate.

1887 The Dawes Act is established, making provisions for allotting tribally held lands to individual Native Americans.

1990 U.S. Census reports Ute population of 7,273.

INDEX

Acknowledgments and Photo Credits
Cover and all artwork by Richard Smolinski
Pages 5, 10, 22, 29, 30: Smithsonian Institution/National Anthropological Archives; pp. 21,
26: ©Blackbirch Press, Inc.
Map by Blackbirch Graphics, Inc.